Wilma Rudolph

by Victoria Sherrow
illustrations by Larry Johnson

M Millbrook Press/Minneapolis

Millbrook Press
A division of Lerner Publishing Group, Inc.
241 First Avenue North
Minneapolis, MN 55401 USA

For reading levels and more information, look up this title at www.lernerbooks.com.

Library of Congress Cataloging-in-Publication Data

Sherrow, Victoria.
  Wilma Rudolph / by Victoria Sherrow; illustrations by Larry Johnson.
    p. cm.—(Carolrhoda on my own books)
  Summary: A biography of the African-American woman who overcame crippling polio as a child to become the first woman to win three gold medals in track in a single Olympics.
  ISBN 978–1–57505–246–5 (lib. bdg. : alk. paper)
  ISBN 978–1–57505–442–1 (pbk. : alk. paper)
  ISBN 978–0–8225–8928–0 (EB pdf)
  1. Rudolph, Wilma, 1940–1995—Juvenile literature.
2. Runners (Sports)—United States—Biography—Juvenile literature. 3. Olympics—Juvenile literature. [1. Rudolph, Wilma, 1940–1995. 2. Track and field athletes.
3. Afro-Americans—Biography. 4. Women—Biography.]
I. Johnson, Larry, 1949– ill. II. Title.
GV1061.15.R83S52 2000
796.42'092—dc21   98-17975
[B]

Manufactured in the United States of America
14 – VI – 3/1/16

For my daughter Caroline, with love—V. S.

It's amazing what hope can accomplish when given long legs and a willing heart. Thank you, Wilma Rudolph.—L. J.

Clarksville, Tennessee

Summer 1946

Wilma Rudolph sat on a hot bus,
looking out the window.
It was 50 long miles to Nashville.

Wilma and her mother
made the trip two times a week.
They went to a hospital there.
Six-year-old Wilma needed help
so she could walk again.

Inside the hospital,

Wilma's mother took the heavy brace

off Wilma's damaged left leg.

A medical student placed the leg

in a tub of warm water.

The student rubbed the weak muscles.

Then came exercises.

Wilma's leg was pushed up and down,

back and forth, and in slow circles.

The exercises hurt.

Tears stung Wilma's eyes.

But she did not give up.

She had been exercising that leg

for two long years.

Hard Years

Wilma had suffered much pain
in her young life.
She was born two months early.
Baby Wilma was so tiny,
the doctors feared she would die.
When Wilma was four years old,
she got very sick with a high fever.
The fever went away,
but she still felt weak.
Wilma's left leg had become
thin and crooked.
Her left foot twisted inward.
"Polio," doctors told her parents.

Polio was a disease that struck
thousands of children each year.
Some died from polio.
Others lost the use of their legs.
It looked like Wilma would have
a difficult future.

Like other black families,
the Rudolphs faced prejudice.
Laws in the South
treated black people unfairly.
Blacks could not sit with whites
in buses, on trains, or in movie theaters.
Black children and white children
went to separate schools.

White doctors took care of white people,
and black doctors took care of
black people.
Only one black doctor
worked in Wilma's town.
The nearest hospital for black people
was in Nashville, more than an hour's
drive away.

Wilma came from a poor family
with 22 children.
Wilma's parents, Ed and Blanche Rudolph,
both had jobs to support
their large family.
Wilma's family had to struggle,
but they had plenty of love.
Together, they felt strong.

No matter how busy
Blanche Rudolph was,
she took Wilma on the long trip
to Nashville.
Wilma watched farms and towns pass by
while she dreamed of a happy future.
She imagined herself walking.
She imagined herself *running*.

Back home, the family helped Wilma
exercise her weak leg.
The Rudolphs knew
Wilma would walk someday.
At last Wilma's hard work paid off.
When she was seven,
she began to walk!
She had a bit of a limp,
and she still wore her leg brace.
But she could finally walk well enough
to go to school.

That first day, Wilma felt lonely.
She watched the other children
run, jump rope, and play ball.
Some of them laughed at her brace.
Wilma felt sad, then mad.
Someday she would be able to run, too.
Someday she would do
something important.

One Sunday when Wilma was 10,
people at her church
got a big surprise.
Wilma walked into church smiling.
Slowly and carefully,
she moved toward her seat.

People stared and whispered.
Wilma Rudolph's leg brace was gone!
But Wilma's fight was not over yet.
She still needed her leg brace
much of the time.
She had to keep exercising.
Then, two years later,
Wilma took off that brace for good.
If she could walk without her brace,
maybe she could run.

Wilma's mind had been busy
all the years she had sat and watched.
She had spent hours at basketball games.
Wilma had studied the players.
She knew all the plays.
She was ready to try.
In high school, Wilma joined
the girls basketball team.
Tall and long legged,
Wilma could *move* on that court!

Although Wilma made the team,
she did not play in many games at first.
But she kept practicing,
sometimes for hours a day.
Her teammates called her Skeeter,
short for mosquito.
The coach said Wilma was everywhere,
"buzzing around like a skeeter."

Finally, Wilma's coach chose her
to be part of the starting team.
In her first big game,
Wilma scored an amazing 32 points.
That year, Wilma's team played
in the state championship game.
Wilma felt sad when they lost.
But a famous college track coach
had been watching her play.
Coach Ed Temple told Wilma
she could be a great runner.

Wilma liked to run,

but she ran just for fun.

She was on the high school track team.

The team did not have a track

to practice on.

Still, Wilma won every race she ran.

Then, at one large track meet,
she did not win a race.
What had gone wrong?
Wilma watched the other runners.
Just running fast was not enough,
she decided.
She would have to learn new skills
if she wanted to be the best.
It was a lesson Wilma never forgot.

Becoming the Best

Ed Temple had not forgotten Wilma.
In 1956, he asked her to spend
the summer at Tennessee State University.
She would train with great track athletes.
That summer, Wilma learned how
to get off to a great start
in a race.
She learned how to
move her arms and legs.
Special exercises
made her stronger and faster.

Wilma tested her new skills
at a big track meet
in Philadelphia, Pennsylvania.
The track field was so large that
Wilma felt tiny.
But she won two races!

Life soon became very exciting
for 16-year-old Wilma.
She was traveling to races
around the country.
Wilma met new people on her travels.

She even got to meet
baseball star Jackie Robinson.
Robinson was the first black man
to play on a major-league baseball team.
Robinson told Wilma
she could be a champion runner.
Wilma later said that
Robinson was "a real hero."

Later that summer,
Wilma went across the country
to Seattle, Washington.
Teams were being chosen
for the 1956 Olympics.
The games would be held
in Melbourne, Australia.
Wilma might have a chance to race
with the best runners
in the world.

Wilma Rudolph ran her best
and earned a spot on the Olympic team!
She was its youngest member.
Before leaving for the Olympics,
Wilma went home to Clarksville.
She had become famous in her hometown.
The town held a ceremony for Wilma.
Her family was proud.

At the Olympic Games,
Wilma had some disappointments.
Only the fastest runners earned a spot
in the final 200-meter race.

She did not run fast enough
to make it to the final race.
Wilma felt sad.
She could not eat or sleep.

Wilma had one more chance
to win a medal.
She was one of four American women
who would run the 400-meter relay race.
The other teams were very fast.
But the Americans won third place!
Wilma had earned a
bronze medal.
She wanted to stand
on the winner's platform again
at the next Olympics.
Wilma thought to herself,
"You've got four years
to get there yourself,
but you've got to
work hard."

After the Olympics,
Wilma went home to Clarksville.
People smiled at her on the street.
They stopped to shake her hand.
Wilma's life returned to normal
for a little while.

She had two years of high school to finish.
After Wilma graduated,
she headed for Tennessee State University.
She joined Ed Temple's track team.
Being on the team was an honor.
And it meant that Wilma
could go to college for free.
Wilma worked hard
and earned good grades.
She also became the fastest runner
on the team.

Olympic Star

By 1960, Wilma was faster than ever.
She made the Olympic team again.
At the Olympics in Rome, Italy,
it was a hot 100 degrees.
The heat did not bother Wilma.
Her mind was on her goal—
to win a gold medal.
She ran on the Olympic grounds
to get ready for her races.

Then disaster struck.

Wilma tripped in a small hole
on the field.

As she fell down,
she felt her ankle pop.

Wilma was worried.

A doctor told Wilma to rest for a few days.

Nobody knew if she would be able to run.

But Wilma was determined.

The races began a few days later.
Wilma felt ready.
She easily reached the finals
of the 100-meter race.
As the final race began,
Wilma pushed herself forward.
She ran with speed and grace.
The fans cheered loudly
as she pulled ahead of the others
and crossed the finish line first.
Smiling joyfully,
Wilma accepted her gold medal.

Later, fans crowded the stands
for the women's 200-meter race.
They wanted to see the runner
who seemed to fly through the air.
Wilma did not disappoint them.
Streaking down the track,
she finished first again.

Fans shouted her name.

Two gold medals for Wilma Rudolph.

By this time, Wilma's ankle hurt.
She tried to ignore it
as the 400-meter relay race began.
Each of her teammates ran 100 meters
carrying a short stick called a baton.
They had to pass the baton quickly
to the next runner in line.
When Wilma's turn came,
the team was in first place.

But Wilma almost dropped the baton.

She lost some speed.

Two runners were ahead of her.

Wilma gathered all her strength.

She set her mind to pass those runners

and pushed her legs forward.

Faster . . . faster . . .

Wilma dashed ahead of the others
and won by less than one second.
She had earned three gold medals.
As Wilma left the victory stand,
a crowd surrounded her.
Photographers snapped pictures
of Olympic champion Wilma Rudolph.
As a child,
Wilma could barely walk.
Just ten years later,
sportswriters called her
"the fastest woman
in the world."
Wilma had dreamed big
and worked hard.
She was a winner
in sports and in life.

Wilma waves to photographers at the 1960 Olympic Games.

Afterword

After the 1960 Olympics, Wilma Rudolph was a hero to people all over the United States. She and her parents were invited to the White House to meet President John F. Kennedy. Wilma gave speeches all over the United States and in other countries. Her warmth and grace impressed people wherever she went.

Wilma retired from racing in 1962, after several more thrilling wins. She finished college in 1963, then taught school and served as a coach. Wilma married and raised two daughters and two sons.

Throughout her life, Wilma spoke out for the things she cared about. She worked to teach sports to children in poor neighborhoods. She hoped that success in sports would help keep children in school. Wilma was happy that her own success had helped women athletes and black athletes.

Wilma died in 1994. Her amazing life continues to inspire people. She once said, "I never forgot all the years when I was a girl and not able to be involved. When I ran, I felt like a butterfly. That feeling was always there."

Important Dates

June 23, 1940—Wilma Rudolph was born in
St. Bethlehem, Tennessee.

1944—Became sick with polio

1947—Started to walk with leg brace

1956—Invited to run at Tennessee State University for the summer; competed in Olympic Games in Melbourne, Australia; won bronze medal in the 400-meter relay race

1958—Started college at Tennessee State University

1960—Competed in Olympic Games in Rome, Italy; won gold medals in the 100-meter race, 200-meter race, and 400-meter relay race

1961—Named Woman Athlete of the Year by Associated Press

1962—Retired from racing

1963—Finished college; married Robert Eldridge

1977—Published *Wilma*, the story she wrote about her life; *Wilma* made into a television movie

1981—Set up Wilma Rudolph Foundation to help amateur athletes

November 12, 1994—Died in Nashville, Tennessee